GARDEN on TOP

Unique ideas for roof gardens | Designing gardens on the highest level | by Barbara P. Meister

CADMOS

Garden design on the highest level

GARDEN on TOP

Imprint

Cadmos Publishing

Copyright © 2012 by
Cadmos Publishing, Richmond
Design: DESIGN.AG, Vienna
Setting: Das Agenturhaus, Munich
Specialist editor:
Barbara P. Meister MA
Translation: Claire Williams

Cover Photographs: Cannes
(Prof. Thomas M. Fürst), Sentosa
(Patrick Bingham Hall), Santiago de
Cuba (DirkvdM – Wikimedia
Commons), Fichtebunker Berlin and
High Line New York (ZinCo GmbH).
Backcover:
Wien (Bernd Hochwartner).
P. 2/3, 5 Prof. Thomas M. Fürst,
P. 7 ZinCo GmbH
Photos within the book originate
from the landscape architects re-
sponsible for the individual projects.
Printing: Werbedruck
Horst Schreckhase GmbH,
Spangenberg

Printed in Germany

ISBN: 978-0-85788-562-3

QR : quick response

With just one click from your smart
phone you can receive further information in a matter of seconds that
you can download, save and use.
QR-Codes replace the need to type
up product advice, information,
domain names and complicated
email addresses.
They save time and reduce the risk of
you copying down the information
incorrectly. Instead of having to copy
the information down, just scan in
the QR-Code.

How to use QR-Codes:
You need a smart phone, tablet-
PC or a notebook with camera
and software (usually via an app)
that reads the QR-Code. The apps
Beetagg and i-nigma are available for mobiles with Apple, Nokia
and Android operating systems.
MacBooks can use Quick Mark for
reading codes or for Windows-
Notebooks zBar is available.

The QR-Code at the end of every
project takes you directly to the
landscape architects' websites.

Foreword

The intellectual inspirations for this book are the biologist and university lecturer, Dr. Bernd Lötsch, and the artist Friedensreich Hundertwasser.

Lötsch was a contributor to the UNESCO Seminars 'Ecosystems Management' and, as a biologist, put forward alternative suggestions for the design of more habitable cities and ways in which traffic problems might be resolved, speaking out against the increasing unsightliness of our cities that is partly due to technocracy. He became better known in Austria from heated television debates about, and giving expert opinions on, current environmental problems.

Hundertwasser created many objects of applied art: designed stamps, flags, coins, porcelain, and also wrote books. From the early 1950s Hundertwasser challenged traditional architecture and advocated a way of designing and constructing buildings that was better both for man and nature. He began his involvement with essays, demonstrations and manifestos such as the 'Mouldiness Manifesto Against Rationalism in Architecture'.

GARDENonTOP is a book about extraordinary roof gardens and features 188 illustrations over 160 pages.

An invitation to take part in this project went out to selected architects, garden landscapers, designers and building contractors worldwide. The invitations were delivered by personal contact, in telephone conversations, letters and emails. The website www.gardenontop.com also provided additional information.

The choice of projects does not represent any form of value judgement. Inclusion in this book and the way a garden is presented was based solely on the quality and quantity of the photos that were provided as well as the project description that accompanied it.

The QR codes take you directly to the relevant web pages of the appropriate garden designer.

The website www.gardenontop.com will continue to provide information about further new developments.

The privacy of all of those involved remains protected. Personal information such as names and addresses of the private clients are not published.

EUROPE

Project: Gene Code Garden |
University Clinic
Landscape architect: club L94
Landschaftsarchitekten GmbH
Photos: Fotoatelier2
Holtschneider & Peetz

Aachen is Germany's westernmost city and has approximately 260,000 inhabitants.
Population density:
1,608 inhabitants/km²

50° 47' N | 6° 5' E
Located at the northern edge of the Eifel. Temperate maritime climate.
Height above sea level:
125–410 metres

The roof gardens and courtyards of Aachen's University Hospital represent a 'microscopic' view of a variety of human and plant components. By centring the gardens in each of their respective courtyards they appear to be framed, thereby emphasising the effect of looking at each of the gardens as if through a microscope.

Regardless of what the surrounding sections and levels are used for, each garden portrays its own unique picture and is accessible for people to walk around. The same paving stones run throughout all of the courtyards as a connecting feature.

The garden themes are interpreted through the use of a combination of different plants, grass, water and materials (gravel, broken glass pieces, wood, etc.). The height of the garden can be varied according to the needs of the plants through the use of raised beds where necessary.

AACHEN
The Gene Code

Project: Gene Code Garden |
University Clinic
Landscape architect: club L94
Landschaftsarchitekten GmbH

The planting depth is set at a minimum of 15 cm, which accommodates the paving stones. All of the themes within the entire landscaped area are interchangeable.

The Gene Code garden was the first of the conceived gardens to be developed, taking the form of a roof garden on the seventh floor of the clinic. It was designed as a representation of man's genetic fingerprint.

The Gene Code garden consists of a series of planting beds designed to resemble barcodes using dark steel alternating with banks, rubbish bins and a play area. They fit into the paving scheme using light grey concrete paving slabs measuring 60 x 40 cm. A lone pine tree adds a special accent to the centre of the courtyard.

The higher beds are planted with monochrome plantings of grasses, yew and dwarf rhododendron using a mulch of basalt gravel. Despite its very formal and structured layout, this actually contributes to creating an extremely diverse, green picture which encourages visitors to sit and enjoy the surroundings.

The red and grey facade of the new clinic is both supported and completed by the green of the plantings.

Photos: Fotoatelier2
Holtschneider & Peetz, Lohmar
Location: Aachen, Germany
www.clubl94.de

Bad Blumau is a community with approximately 1,700 inhabitants located in the eastern part of Styria, about 10 kilometres north of the regional capital of Fürstenfeld.
Population density:
43 inhabitants/km²

47° 7' N | 16° 3' E
In the hills of the eastern part of Styria: Pannonian climate (warm and dry).
Height above sea level: 284 metres

Grassed-over roofs, curved and rounded forms, colourful facades, golden domes and colours that are reminiscent of a rainbow surrounded by fields and pastures all combine to create a living work of art. It clearly shows the stamp of the artist Friedensreich Hundertwasser and reflects his philosophy: life in harmony with nature.

The Rogner thermal spa and health resort in Bad Blumau is laid out in four irregular quarters. The ring-shaped inner thermal area forms the centre with the irregularly shaped living, bathing and restaurant areas branching out from the centre into the open landscaped areas beyond.

More than 330 pillars and 2,400 windows of different shapes and sizes offer a unique trip of discovery.

'On a rainy day colours really begin to glow', said the painter Friedensreich Hundertwasser, 'that is why a gloomy day – a rainy day – is actually for me the best type of day. It is a day on which I can work. When it rains I am happy. And when it rains I know that my day can begin!

'Nature, art and creation are all the same thing. It is us that have separated them out. If we abuse nature's creation and if we destroy our own innate creative ability then we destroy ourselves ... Here we have created a new landscape. In principle, everything that is horizontal and in the open belongs to nature. Here this is put into practice. Man is nature's guest and should behave as such. Here too this is realised. You can walk over wooded hills and be surprised to discover that people are living beneath you.'

Excerpt from a communication from Friedensreich Hundertwasser to Rogner, Bad Blumau.

Project: Bad Blumau, Rogner Therme
Architect: Robert Rogner,
Friedensreich Hundertwasser

The town of Bad Vilbel, with its 32,000 inhabitants, borders the northern edge of the city of Frankfurt am Main.
Population density:
1,241 inhabitants/km²

50° 11′ N | 8° 44′ E
Located between Taunus and Vogelsberg: moderate, sometimes mild climate with katabatic winds (winds that blow down from higher elevations) and colder air streams coming from the Taunus mountain range.
Height above sea level: 109 metres

Linear, vertical and geometric shapes and elements are what give this roof garden its character. The generous terraced area has been decked with oak planks.

Two steps and two 15 cm deep pools made from stainless steel separate the garden from the seating area that is set on a higher level. At night this area is illuminated by light cubes. The pools can be crossed on flat lava-basalt stepping stones. One of the pools is planted with mare's tail *(Equisetum)*. To reinforce the straight lines, raised beds have been planted with lines of lavender, roses, grasses, herbs and box. Existing trees, including hornbeam *(Carpinus)*, red gum *(Liquidambar)* and an apple tree, were all incorporated into the design.

Project: Minimalism
Landscape Architect: Ute Wittich
Garden Architecture, Frankfurt/Main
Photos: Ute Wittich
Location: Bad Vilbel
www.utewittich.de

BAD VILBEL
Minimalism

BERLIN
Fichtebunker

With 3.45 million inhabitants, Germany's capital, Berlin, has the highest population density of any city in Germany and is the second largest city in the European Union.
Population density:
3,902 inhabitants/km²

52° 29' 25" N | 13° 24' 45" E
Situated in the Warsaw-Berlin glacial valley on the River Spree: moderate climate on the border of where the climate changes from a maritime to a continental one.
Height above sea level: 34–115 metres

The 'Fichtebunker' in the Kreuzberg district of Berlin has a diameter of 56 metres and is 27 metres high. It is the only remaining brick gasometer left in Berlin.

Under the steel cupola of what was also used as an air-raid shelter, there are now twelve two-storey condominiums that have been built around the circular roof making up the exclusive housing development known as the 'Circle houses', each with its own garden and a view of the city. The building itself is under heritage protection. This is an example of how modern living and high-quality garden design can be combined with a listed property – even when it is a roof.

The circular building is topped by a 'Schwedler Cupola', an unsupported steel vault comprising radial rafters, crossbeams, crossed with diagonal draw rods and named after its designer, the building engineer Johann Wilhelm Schwedler (1823–1894).

Due to the huge foundations and a 3-metre thick concrete and steel roof, there were no problems with the proposed load; however, ensuring that the Schwedler Cupola was unaffected posed a logistical problem during the construction and building works. All of the material that was required for the building site on the roof had to be lifted in through the cupola opening with a crane.

The challenge for the architect was ensuring that modern architecture worked in harmony with the history of the building.

High-quality planting played an important role in this building project. Every apartment had its own private garden. These gardens have a size of between 68 and 170 m² and are located between the apartment and the edge of the roof. Due to the restrictions imposed by the listed status of the building, no high trees or climbing plants were permitted as these might have damaged the cupola. The ZinCo system 'Heather with Lavender' was used as the substrate basis for the various plantings which utilises Flora-drain FD 40 water retention and drainage elements.
This 40 mm deep drainage layer retains rain water in troughs on the upper side whilst the surplus water is safely drained away underneath. For this drainage system to work without any complications, however, a number of tapping holes had to be drilled through the roof of the bunker and be connected with the bunker's main drainage system.

Three different garden designs with the appropriate plants were developed, taking into account the extreme conditions of wind and sun that the plants would have to withstand due to their location on a roof. The favourite design was the Japanese style garden.

Following modern trends, evergreen plants such as Morrow's sedge and sheep's fescue grass were selected. Added to these were pines and maple trees as well as further robust and easy-growing ground coverage, such as the cushion bolax (Azorella), Irish moss and thyme.

For the shrub and flower gardens lavender, hollyhocks, delphinium, cranesbill and summer lilac were chosen.

Project: Berlin –
Circle houses on the Fichtebunker
Green roof construction:
ZinCo GmbH
Architect: Ingenbleek GmbH
Architekten
Landscape Architect:
verde-gartengestaltung
Photos: ZinCo GmbH, Kessler
(photo at night, pages 24/25)
www.zinco-greenroof.com

BUTZBACH
Fallen Leaves

Butzbach is a town in the state of Hessen with around 25,000 inhabitants located in the district of Wetterau.
Population density:
234 inhabitants/km²

The aims of this project were both to put on new roof insulation as well as to create additional space for employees to use for smaller meetings and also to give them space to take breaks and to have their lunch outside in the open.

50° 26' N | 8° 40' E
Located on the north-east border between Taunus and Wetterau: cool, humid uplands climate.
Height above sea level: 199 metres

The building's location is subject to continuous wind for the entire year. The leaves that are being constantly blown in from the surrounding vegetation were the inspiration for the designer's decision to reflect the falling of leaves on the roof itself. Leaves of various sizes were laid out on the differently proportioned areas of the roof, creating an unmistakable design.

The almost square cafeteria garden is divided into six leaves in an open-air room immediately opposite the entrance and includes a secluded area around a circular water tray.

The cafeteria terrace is used flexibly and required a mobile screen to add to its privacy. The glass fibre sticks that have been inserted into rubber blocks fulfil this purpose and harmonise well with the planting. They also create the impression of over-sized grasses. The oblong roof gardens wind almost scarf-like around the building. The leaves 'dance' across the various spaces and allow room for shady trees. Open 'leaves' framed by hedges form quiet areas that can be used to retreat into.

For the extensive plantings of shrubs and grasses, a 15 cm-deep planting mulch was laid down as a base. In the raised 'leaf' beds planted partly with trees and shrubs a substrate of 30 centimetres in depth was used. All planted areas are irrigated by an automated system during the growing season.

The garden is now five years old. Two long and snowy winters have had their effect. The trees and shrubs that were chosen are growing and developing as was hoped and they are already having the intended effect.

Specimen trees and shrubs: Juneberry *(Amelanchier lamarckii)*, ginnala maple *(Acer ginnala)*, witch alder *(Fothergilla gardenii)*, witch hazel *(Hamamelis of different varieties)*, Fothergilla *(Fothergilla major)*, winged spindle tree *(Euonymus alatus)*, honeysuckle *(Lonicera maackii)*, Japanese crab apple *(Malus floribunda)*, crab apple *(Malus sylvestris)*, autumn flowering cherry *(Prunus subhirtella 'Autumnalis')*, common lilac *(Syringa vulgaris)*, pagoda tree *(Cornus alterniflora)*, wedding cake tree *(Cornus controversa)*.

Hedges: Common maple *(Acer campestre)*, common beech *(Fagus sylvatica)*, yew *(Taxus baccata)*.

Shrubs, flowers and grasses: Lady's mantle *(Alchemilla mollis)*, stonecrop *(Sedum)*, barrenwort *(Epimedium)*, sword grass *(Miscanthus)*, Japanese anemone *(Anemone japonica)*, evening primrose *(Oenothera missouriensis)*, Michaelmas daisy *(Aster laevis, Aster pansus 'Snowflurry')*, moor grass *(Molinia)*, bergenia *(Bergenia)*, plantain lily *(Hosta)*, peach-leaved bellflower *(Campanula persicifolia)*, bugbane *(Cimicifuga)*, cranesbill *(Geranium)*, day lily *(Hemerocallis)*, iris *(Iris barbata)*, peony *(Paeonia lactiflora)*, pachysandra *(Pachysandra 'Green Carpet')*, feather reed grass *(Calamagrostis brachytricha)*, great wood-rush *(Luzula sylvatica 'Snow Bunny')*.

Project: Fallen Leaves,
Hess Nature's Roof Garden
Landscape architect:
Büro Keller & Keller
Landschaftsarchitekten
Photos: Rainer Keller, Petra Keller
Location: Butzbach in Hessen
www.kellerundkeller.de

CANNES
Le Cannet

Cannes is a city with nearly 75,000 inhabitants in the South of France in the Alpes-Maritimes Département. Population density:
3,718 inhabitants/km²

Following the purchase of a rooftop apartment in a popular area of Cannes – Le Cannet – located above the Old City, the new owner sought to redesign the rather bleak and uninviting roof area that was both open and overlooked on all sides, turning it into a much more usable space.

43° 33′ N | 7° 1′ E
South-west of the Southern French Alps along the Côte d'Azur: Mediterranean climate.
Height above sea level: 8 metres (0–260 m)

In redesigning the rooftop garden the aim was to create a unique and distinctive roof landscape that offered privacy and protected against prying eyes while making the most of the wide-ranging views over the bay of Cannes.

The garden was to reflect the Mediterranean character of its setting but also strike out in new directions and create an area that was both exciting and scintillating.

The extreme climatic conditions that prevailed – sea air and strong sun – made the choice of plants and building materials more difficult.

In this project a special type of render for use on aluminium building components was developed. All pieces were prefabricated exactly to the right shape and size in Germany so that the construction time on site was reduced to a minimum.

By putting multiple layers of the render onto each of the individual segments and the walls, a practical and yet vivid texture was created.

The colours chosen for the landscaping and planters are an integral part of the total concept of the design and unite as one with the surrounding natural stone, the wood and the wide array of plants.

Palms, olives, citrus trees, bougainvillea, jasmine and cypresses form a dense screen and protect the area from outside view.

The implementation of this project was much more complicated and took much more time than it would have done had the project been in Germany due to the special nature of the site, the local planning challenges and the necessity of coordinating with a contractor that was in Germany.

The uniqueness of this roof garden lies in the custom-made metal building elements, the variety of ways in which natural stone is used, the fully automated sun sails, the use of local Mediterranean plants, as well as the implementation of a concept whereby the light can be directed and controlled.

Project: Cannes Roof Garden
Landscape architect: Prof. Thomas M. Fürst, Sebastian Fürst,
FÜRST Architects GmbH, Düsseldorf
Photos: Prof. Thomas M. Fürst
Location: Cannes, France, Europe
www.fuerst-architects.com

CASCAIS
Estoril Sol

The Portuguese town of Cascais with around 34,000 inhabitants lies about 25 km west of Lisbon.
Population density:
1,659 inhabitants/km²

38° 42' N | 9° 25' W
On the Atlantic coast: semi-humid and maritime climate, sub-tropical zone.
Height above sea level: 0–25 metres

Estoril Sol Residences: a modern building complex with 100 apartments located close to the Atlantic coast. The challenge in carrying out this project was to give the enormous scale of the building a more human and pleasing scale through the use of extensive plantings.

The garden is on the roof of an underground garage and is formed using a tunnel system which connects the apartment towers with each other underground garage. The roof garden stretches over an area of 9,000 m². The plants chosen had to be saline-resistant since the wind coming off the Atlantic constantly carried sea salt with it.

The path was lined with fan palms *(Washingtonia filifera)* in curved planting containers. These containers were made from Corten steel, a copper, nickel and chromium alloy of weathered steel. The smoothness of this material enabled the wave-like shapes of the containers to be easily produced. In addition, its rusty brown colour blended in well with the planting.

A part of the design concept for the 15-metre-wide path is a 4-metre-wide water channel, running along the length of the building's façade, which helps to protect the residents' privacy. It is an important part of the design that has a positive effect on both temperature and humidity, especially during the hot summer months.

The surface of the water channel itself is finished using traditional Portuguese Calçada-Mosaic tiles. The pattern pays homage to the sun and is a reminder of the famous old Estoril Sol hotel that once stood on the same site.

In the dense planting can be found stone pine *(Pinus pinea)*, combined with the grey foliage and blue flowers of the Pride of Madeira *(Echium candicans)*. Trees could be planted once the depth of the planting beds was increased to 1.2 metres thanks to the Corten steel walls.

Project: Estoril Sol Residences
Landscape architects:
Francisco Manuel Caldeira Cabral,
Elsa Maria Matos Severino –
Gabinete de Arquitectura Paisagista
Photos: Francisco Manuel Caldeira Cabral
Location: Cascais, Portugal
www.franciscocaldeiracabral.com

FRANKFURT
Bürgerhospital

The Hessian metropolis of Frankfurt-am-Main, with its population of around 680,000, is the fifth largest city in Germany. It counts as one of the 'Alpha word cities' and is thus one of the most significant cities in the world.

Population density:
2,737 inhabitants/km²

50° 7′ 50″ N | 8° 41′ 10″ E
Located at the northern end of the upper Rhine Valley in one of the warmest parts of Germany: warm and temperate rainy climate.
Height above sea level: 112 metres

The Frankfurt Bürgerhospital is located in the densely populated district of Nordend-West. The hospital's lack of green spaces at ground level has been supplemented by a colourful garden on the roof for now more than ten years and spreads over 750 m². Employees enjoy using the garden in their breaks and patients enjoy relaxing and recuperating in the fresh air.

In the course of a rebuild in 2008, the roof garden was completely dismantled and then completely reassembled with the exact same design two storeys higher up. The well-proven ZinCo-Systembau substrate system was incorporated into the relocated garden using the Floradrain FD 60 water retention and drainage system.

The raised beds show an ever-changing flowering picture over the entire year. Even in winter the viburnum *(Viburnum x bodnantense)* flowers. In autumn the heavily scented fragrant olive *(Osmanthus)* makes a real impression and, just like the lilac *(Syringa)*, is real proof that this roof garden stimulates the senses in more ways than one.

The sense of touch is also not left out thanks to a small track with different surfaces which is intended for diabetics and allows the walker's feet to feel warm and cold and hard and soft surfaces.

Climbing trellises of roses attract the attention whilst at the same time hiding the air ventilation pipes that come out onto the roof: a functional and creative solution. Individual bushes as high as 3 metres, such as juneberry *(Amelanchier)*, give added emphasis to the design. Clematis *(Clematis)* and the evergreen honeysuckle *(Lonicera henryi)* improve the look of the adjoining facade and help to add to the entire harmonious picture created by the roof garden.

Project: Bürgerhospital
Green roof construction:
ZinCo GmbH
Landscape planning: Peter Vaughan
Photos: ZinCo GmbH
Location: Frankfurt-am-Main
www.zinco-greenroof.com

Sittard-Geleen is an industrial town with around 97,000 inhabitants in the south of the Dutch province of Limburg.
Population density:
1,214 inhabitants/km²

51° 1' N | 5° 52' E
Maritime climate with cool winters and mild summers.
Height above sea level: 67 metres

Il Giardino is situated in the centre of the Geleen district. The landscape typical of this part of the country comprises shelter belts, sunken roads and patchworks of fields and waterways. Visitors to this garden find a modern interpretation of classic form. They follow meandering paths bordered by flowering shrubs, flower beds, well laid lawns and quiet stretches of water.

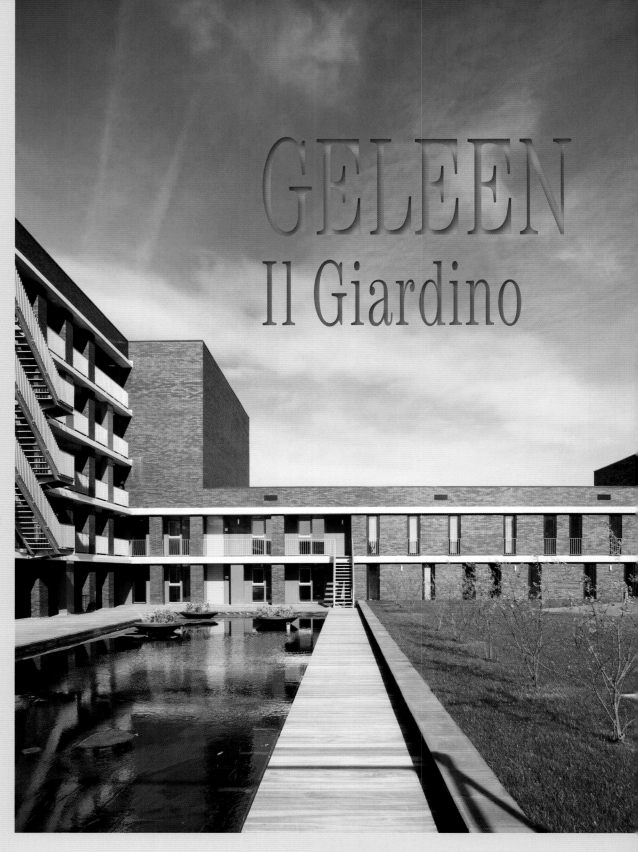

GELEEN
Il Giardino

The roof garden forms a convenient inner courtyard for the 66 apartments around it. It measures 60 x 35 m and was built on the roof of a shopping centre. Apart from the structural demands that accompany a roof garden of this proportion, the other considerations were allowing for accommodation of large quantities of rainwater and ensuring that the garden was low maintenance.

The modern materials used, such as the Corten steel for the paths and galvanised steel for the pergolas, integrate as one with the surrounding buildings.

Project: Il Giardino, Market in Geleen
Landscape architect:
Atelier Pieroen-Hoffman
Photos: Jaqueline Hoffman,
Philip Driessen
Location:
Sittard-Geleen, The Netherlands
www.pieroen-hoffman.nl

LEER
Zen Garten

The district capital of Leer in Lower Saxony, with a population of 34,000 inhabitants, is the third largest city in Eastern Friesland.
Population density:
488 inhabitants/km²

53° 14' N | 7° 27' E
The clients had returned to Germany after living in the Japanese capital, Tokyo, for 25 years. They had grown so fond of their adopted country of Japan that they didn't want to totally abandon Japanese culture in their 'old new' home town of Leer.

The clients had really treasured and appreciated their time in Japan and so it seemed obvious to design a garden that would remind them of this faraway culture.

Thus it was decided to design and construct a Zen-styled garden (Kare-sansui) on the roof terrace of their newly built two-storey penthouse.

Due to the proximity to the coast, the coastal wind, called a 'light breeze' by the locals, presented real problems for plants located on a roof. Pine trees, formed into outdoor bonsai, tolerated the constant movement of the air. Also included were azaleas, grasses and rounded box.

What emerged was a design that, while not blocking the view over Leer, at the same time directed it through the Zen garden, constantly recalling memories of the client's former home in Japan.

The house itself is situated in the middle of the harbour basin in the historic town of Leer (Lower Saxony) where sailing ships of almost every size are moored.

The charm of this design is the way in which it links a historic Lower Saxony harbour town with the Far Eastern appeal of a Japanese garden's aesthetics. The design is often complemented by the large sailing boats whose masts match or even exceed the height of the pine trees on the terrace.

Project: Zen Garden on a roof terrace in Leer
Design: Dr. Wolfgang Hess, Japan Garten Kultur, Liebenau
Photos: Dr. Wolfgang Hess
Location: Leer
www.japan-garten-kultur.de

With its 190,000 inhabitants Linz, the provincial capital of Upper Austria, is the third largest city in Austria.
Population density:
1.973 inhabitants/km²

48° 18' N, 14° 17' E
Located in the Linz basin on the Danube: combining a sub-oceanic and sub-continental climate.
Height above sea level: 266 metres

Slightly raised and well-defined beds were individually planted out with groups of grasses, lavender and perennials. Box hedging and a centrally located lavender bed give the garden's structure clear definition.
A gently winding garden path leads the way through themed areas with what appears to be natural contours and terracing.

The clinic's elegant roof terrace was to feature an easy to maintain garden that offered flowering highlights throughout the whole year. The specification allowed for a minimum height and so a roof garden was created that featured themed planting beds. It creates an interesting and vibrant picture over the entire year.

Project: More Garden
Landscape architect: Markus Lindinger-Hofmann, KriegerGut Garten- und Landschaftsdesign
Photos: Johanna Heiligenbrunner
Location: Linz
www.kriegergut.at

LINZ
More Garden

London is the capital of both England and the United Kingdom. The city lies on the River Thames in the South-East of England. Approximately 7,825,000 people live in Greater London.
Population density:
4,758 inhabitants/km²

51° 29' 34'' N | 0° 13' 33'' W
The location lies under the influence of the Atlantic Gulf Stream and has a temperate climate. In winter the temperature rarely drops under 0°C (32°F).
Height above sea level: 15 metres

Hammersmith in the west of London is not particularly well known for its green spaces. However, when you look a little closer in between the concrete and the flyovers you can see a small patch of green.

The new attraction at the Lyric Theatre isn't a show, but rather a roof garden with flowering magnolia trees, eucalyptus, Chinese wisteria and clematis, together with an Italian café, pergolas and well-designed lighting for the evenings. The garden was developed on the first floor of the Lyric Theatre overlooking the Lyric Square and King Street.

LONDON
Lyric Theatre

The client wanted to create a green landmark amongst an urban concrete jungle and the new green space had to be accessible for the locals.

The roof terrace, located eight metres above street level, was totally refurbished. The new wooden flooring and cladding, the low planters, lamps and the six-metre-high pergolas can all be seen from the Hammersmith underground station.

More than 16 tonnes of topsoil, 15 tonnes of building timber and 2 tonnes of sheet steel were used during construction of the garden. 750 trees, shrubs, perennials and 3 fully grown eucalyptus trees were planted out.

From an ecological point of view, this project is a step in the right direction. The roof garden absorbs up to 75 percent of the rain water that falls. Water that falls under the terrace flooring is collected and then used to water the plants. The combination of plants, incorporating as they do indigenous species, provide an essential habitat for bird and insect populations.

Concrete and asphalt cities store heat and become urban 'heat oases', the temperature of which typically tends to be up to 5°C higher than in the suburbs. Roof gardens can therefore have a positive effect on the urban climate. Through transpiration the plants help to cool the air, thus reducing the temperature over the surface of the terrace.

Up to 85 percent of the particles in the air are bound to a leaf's upper surface. In the winter the dissipation of heat from the building underneath the roof garden is reduced by up to 30 percent and in summer the rooms stay cooler.

To protect the roof area the entire surface was covered with watertight, environmentally sound sheeting. The garden will extend the lifespan of the roof structure by 70 percent.

The garden is a popular place and is enjoyed by many – by actors preparing themselves for a performance, by children on school outings and by mothers with infants.

Project: Lyric Theatre Roof Garden
Landscape architect:
Davies White Landscape Architects
Photos:
Davies White Landscape Architects
Location: Lyric Theatre,
Hammersmith, London
www.davieswhite.co.uk

LONDON
Monaco Garden

As part of the Chelsea Flower Show, Sarah Eberle brought the flora typical of the sun-drenched principality of Monaco to London. 'A Monaco Garden' characterised the interaction between architecture and Monaco's natural landscape.

The garden reflected a sustainable solution to the question of how to design an exclusive-looking green space in a densely populated area by the greening up of surfaces that tend to be otherwise ignored. Vertical green walls are just as much a part of the plan as the roof garden planted out with lavender that is reached via a balcony. Space-saving, vertical gardens were created using succulent varieties of Hottentot Fig *(Carpobrotus edulis)* and orange flowering Cape daisies *(Osteospermum)*.

The other plants of this garden are also suited to Monaco's Mediterranean location, for example, the carob tree *(Ceratonia siliqua)*, succulents *(Lampranthus in different varieties)*, silk floss tree *(Ceiba speciosa)*, black pine *(Pinus nigra)*, tree aloe *(Aloe barberae)* and mandarin trees *(Citrus reticulata)*.

Project: A Monaco Garden
Landscape architect: Sarah Eberle
Photos: Sarah Eberle
Location: Chelsea Flower Show
www.saraheberle.com

The Cromwell Tower was, at the time of its completion in 1973, the highest building in Europe and even today it is still amongst the highest in London. The triangular skyscraper lies on the corner of Beech and Silk Streets within London's Square Mile.

51° 31' 13'' N | 0° 05' 33'' W
The large observation platform on the 38th floor offers a breathtaking view over the city's famous landmarks.

LONDON
Landmarks

Beech *(Betula)* and ginkgo trees *(Ginkgo biloba)* cope very well with the extreme conditions that prevail at this elevated height.

Hard-wearing Lapacho wood *(Tabebuia ipe, Green Ironwood, Ipé)* was used for the platform's flooring.

Project: Cromwell Tower
Landscape architect:
Amir Schlezinger, MyLandscapes
Photos:
Amir Schlezinger, Richard Gaunt
Location: London, Cromwell Tower
www.mylandscapes.co.uk

Cromwell Tower

The Grosvenor Canal in Pimlico was opened in 1825. In 2000 planning permission was granted for the construction of a modern apartment complex – Grosvenor Waterside. The canal after which it is named no longer exists.

51° 29' 11" N | 0° 8' 57" W
This roof garden lies in the City of Westminster located in London's south-west.

A variety of flooring is used to tone in with the varying architectural surroundings – quarry tiles to echo Ken Shuttleworth's Bramah building in the background, hardwood flooring in brown tones to tone with Chelsea Bridge.

Two seating areas invite the visitor to enjoy the most fantastic of views – out towards nearby Battersea Power Station and to the London landmarks of Big Ben and the London Eye.

Pine trees, birch and olives cope well with the windy conditions and the strong sun. The clear, strong lines of the imposing agaves serve to emphasise the architectural design.

Project: Grosvenor Waterside
Landscape architect:
Amir Schlezinger, MyLandscapes
Photos: Amir Schlezinger
www.mylandscapes.co.uk

Grosvenor Waterside

The modern building complex of St. George Wharf lies on the Thames riverbank in Vauxhall, London.

51° 29' 08'' N | 0° 07' 37'' W
Immediately adjacent to the Thames, this 220 m² roof garden is located on the seventh floor of this unmistakable building built in the shape of a ship's bow.

The garden has a direct relationship with the roof architecture and the structures, textures and colours of its surroundings.
The panoramic view is framed by low planting that draws a distinct boundary to the dramatic backdrop. When choosing plants, particular value was placed on low maintenance. Ornamental grasses and the imposing agave cope well with the perpetual wind that comes off the river.
There is an inbuilt sound and public address system for entertainers and for the guests there is a mini golf course on the upper terrace. In the evening a discreet lighting system ensures a congenial atmosphere.

Project: St. George Wharf
Landscape architect: Amir Schlezinger, MyLandscapes
Photos: Amir Schlezinger, Tim Soar
Location: London, Vauxhall
www.mylandscapes.co.uk

St. George Wharf

LONDON
Sloane Square

Sloane Square in London lies between the elegant districts of Knightsbridge, Belgravia and Chelsea.
Population density:
4,758 inhabitants/km²

51° 29' 33" N | 0° 9' 26" W
Under the influence of the Gulf-Stream: temperate climate with warm summers and cool winters; it is rare for the temperature to fall below freezing. In the centre of the city the temperatures are often up to 5°C higher than in the suburbs of London.
Height above sea level: 15 metres

This L-shaped roof terrace in Sloane Square in the heart of London was designed to link the interior and exterior spaces in the best way possible.

The terrace is reached through two folding doors. The floor levels of the interior and exterior living areas were adjusted to match. When the doors are opened, two large L-shaped sofas – one inside and one outside – create a comfortable U-shaped seating area facing an outdoor fireplace and an indoor television.

An additional bench made from cedar wood was installed on the edge of a small watercourse. Tucked away behind a planting of birch, grasses and lavender, this part of the garden is virtually hidden and is perfectly suited to quiet relaxation in the evening.

Western red cedar *(Thuja plicata)* has proven to be a hard-wearing and robust wood for the outside areas.

The planting is dominated by Himalayan birch *(Betula utilis* var. *jacquemontii)*. The undergrowth features perennials and grasses such as anemone *(Anemone x hybrida* 'Honorine Jobert'), feather reed grass *(Calamagrostis x acutiflora* 'Karl Foerster' and 'Overdam'), Lindheimer's beeblossom *(Gaura lindheimeri)*, New Zealand satin flower *(Libertia grandiflora)*, Chinese silver grass *(Miscanthus sinensis* 'Gracillimus'), catnip *(Nepeta' faassenii* 'Six Hills Giant'), millet *(Panicum virgatum)*, pheasant tail grass *(Stipa arundinacea)*, Mexican feather grass *(S. tenuissima)*, verbena *(Verbena rigida)*, tussock grass *(Deschampsia cespitosa* 'Tauträger') and lavender *(Lavandula angustifolia)*.

Project: Chelsea Roof Garden
Landscape architect:
Philip Woodburn, Fork Garden Design
Photos: Philip Woodburn
Location: Chelsea, London
www.forkgardendesign.com

The Spanish capital of Madrid, with its 3,273,050 inhabitants, is the third largest city in the European Union.
Population density:
5,403 inhabitants/km²

40° 24' N | 3° 42' W
Continental climate: hot, dry summers and relatively cold winters.
Height above sea level: 650 metres

The design was intentionally kept simple and clean. It was to form an easy to care for and quiet green space that is predominantly used for reading.
The tree sculpture from rusted steel plays the leading role in this company. Positioned on a metal plinth at eye level, it demands the observer's full attention.

The planting too was reduced to the basics. New Zealand flax *(Phormium tenax)*, with its imposing, sword-like leaves, forms a green frame around the garden. Box *(Buxus sempervirens)* trimmed into squares breaks up the uniform limestone tiled floor. Furniture, planters and the back wall immediately behind the sculpture are all made from woven poly-rattan.

Project: Brick-walled Garden
Landscape architect: Jesús Ibáñez
Photo: Ignacio Uribesalazar Artázcoz
Location: Madrid, Altstadt
www.jesusibanez.com

MADRID
Brick Garden

MADRID
Family Rooftop

With 3,273,050 inhabitants Spain's capital Madrid is the European Union's third largest city. The suburb of Santa Barbara is located in the centre of the city.
Population density:
5,403 inhabitants/km²

40° 25' 28'' N | 3° 41' 38'' W
Continental climate with hot and dry summers and winters that are, for Spain, relatively cool.
Height above sea level: 667 metres

In the middle of the city centre there is an old pre-World War II building, from the roof of which one can enjoy a fantastic view over the city. The challenge of this project was to transform the old roof terrace into a place of relaxation and reflection.

All members of the family were to have their own space, and there was a requirement for a safe play area for the children as well.

There was already a low maintenance roof garden in place that could be used around the clock for everyday family life and as a play area. The existing building structure and location of the fireplace helped in dividing the space into individually themed areas.

A generously sized area for relaxation was covered by a pergola that offers protection from the sun in the hot summer months. The barbeque area offers space for cooking and eating. In the spa area there is a shower and corner pool to help to cool off.

The children's play area was fully integrated into the design and surrounded by tall containers that prevent anyone from climbing the wall.

The rubber resin flooring mats also offer good protection in case of falls.

For evenings and nights, well-thought-out lighting, a fountain and hi-fi system all ensure that parties are a real experience.

Project: Urban Rooftop Garden
Landscape architect: Juan Casla
Photos: Luis H. Segovia
Location:
Santa Barbara, Madrid, Spanien
www.caslajardineria.com

MADRID
Mirror

With 3,273,050 inhabitants Spain's capital Madrid is the European Union's third largest city
Population density:
5,403 inhabitants/km²

40° 25' N | 3° 42' W
Continental climate with hot and dry summers and winters that are, for the Spanish at least, relatively cool.
Height above sea level: 667 metres

This private roof garden in the historic part of the city stretches over two levels. The challenge facing the landscape architect was to transform a roof terrace that had seen better days into a modern space that balanced with the contrast of its historical city surroundings. Thus, an inviting and functional open-air space was created from an impersonal terrace.

A key aspect of the design was incorporating the existing balustrade and parapet into the concept and enhancing it by combining it with vertical panels.

A wall-shaped black slate fountain forms the central point of the vertically panelled area, flanked on both sides by the elegant shape of two weeping cedars.

The square area of lawn in the centre forms an optical anchor of calm that is framed with wood.
The terrace is surrounded with dark grey planters placed on a bed of grey gravel.

The formal austerity of the containers is relieved by plantings of fine feather grass *(Stipa tenuissima)*.

The double-walled metal planters allow for the integrated installation of a modern lighting system which, at twilight and in the evenings, gives the garden an especially exclusive feel. The lighting is continued into the vertical alongside the fountain and thus strengthens the effect. In addition, the upright lighting strips serve to accentuate the natural stone surfaces.

Great value was placed on the optical effect that the lighting was to create. It begins at dusk in a warm yellow tone and as it gets darker changes into a cooler white.

As you walk onto the terrace from the living area, the visitor's attention focuses on the historic surroundings and the imposing looking fountain, whilst the stairs and the upper terrace remain virtually unnoticed. The guest is then offered a further surprise when he enters the upper terrace via the steps and a peaceful garden room under Madrid's blue sky is revealed. This quiet haven invites you to relax or sunbathe without disturbance. But parties too are held here. Lone trees, palms and strelitzia stamp their character on this roof terrace. At dusk the borders of the illuminat-ed garden melt into the brick-coloured roof landscape of the surrounding old town and the sunset on the horizon.

Project: Mirrors the sky in Spain
Landscape architect:
Fernando Pozuelo Corral – Fernando Pozuelo landscaping collection
Photos: Luis Benolier
Location: Madrid, Spain
www.fernandopozuelo.com

After London and Berlin Madrid is the third largest city in the European Union.

40° 24' N | 3° 42' W
Due to its altitude and the continental climate, it has hot, dry summers and relatively cold winters.
Height above sea level: 650 metres

Symmetry and geometric forms are the quintessential elements of this roof garden as they occur recurrently in both the vertical and horizontal. A modern, white sculptured fountain forms the focal point of the garden.

The strict use of form creates a clear and calm impression. In order that the formal concept can be maintained over time, low-maintenance box *(Buxus sempervirens)* which can also cope with frequent trimming, was used in the design of the areas. The garden is accessible directly from the house's main hall. A part of the open space is also used as a shaded seating area.

Project: Sky Garden
Landscape architect: Jesús Ibáñez
Photos:
Ignacio Uribesalazar Artázcoz
Location: Centre of Madrid
www.jesusibanez.com

MADRID
Sky Garden

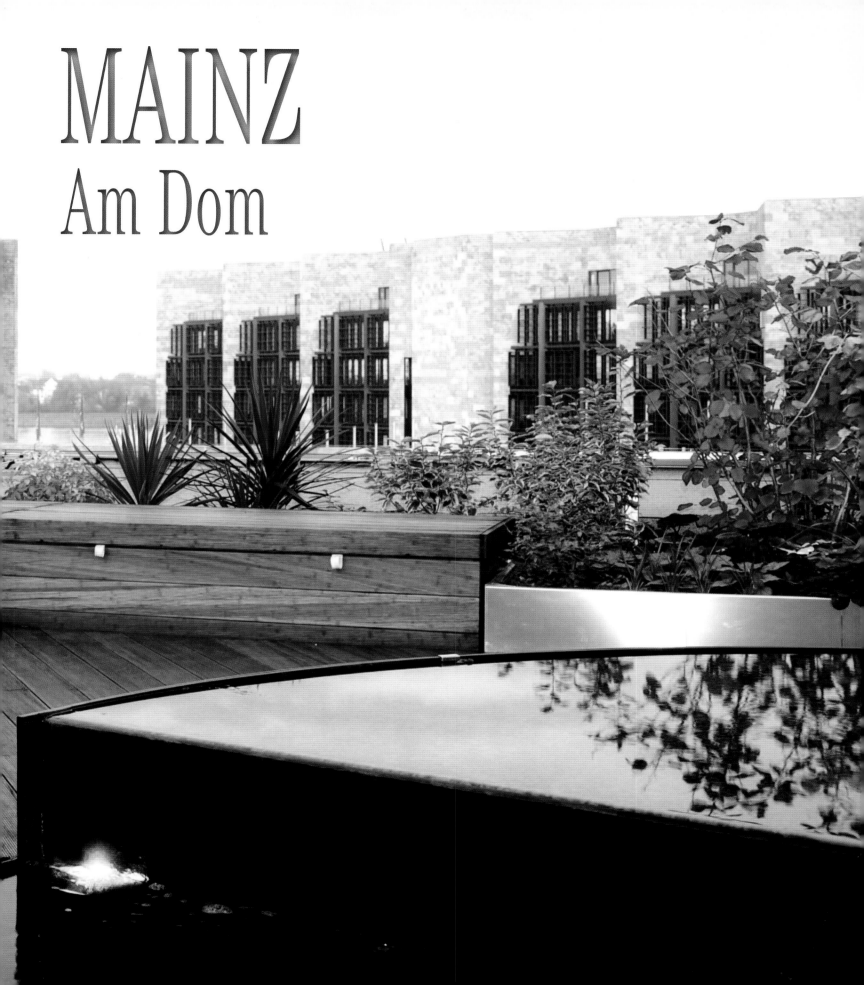

MAINZ
Am Dom

Mainz is the capital of the German state of Rheinland-Pfalz and, with 199,237 inhabitants, is also the largest city in the state.
Population density:
2,038 inhabitants/km²

50° 0' N | 8° 16' E
Well-known wine area with an almost semi-arid climate.
Height above sea level: 88 metres

The idea for creating a stylish roof garden near to Mainz cathedral came about after a department store and its roof were substantially renovated. What was special about this project, however, was that two parties were involved, both of whom had their own suggestions and ideas for the spaces available: the building's owner and the new tenant. The latter wanted a show garden in which new types of plants could be presented. It needed to be designed for comfort and used for recreational purposes, with water, areas for stretching out and relaxing, without the need of additional furnishing. Light flooring material and differing levels of plantings as well as space for meetings with customers and events were all part of the brief.

In the meditation garden, which is bordered and framed by bamboo, particular attention was placed on the 'eye of light'. This oval-shaped

glazed-over area affords a special atmosphere when it is dark thanks to the remote-controlled LED light strips set in through the sides of the glass.

In autumn the restrained planting of dark conifers, white flowering heather and ferns act as a counterpoint to the spherical Japanese maple when it puts on its magnificent orange-red mantle. One of the areas is brought to life by intensely coloured plants such as the dark leaved alumroot and the green and red striped grasses.

The spotlights that are barely noticeable during the day create a wonderful atmosphere in the evening and put the plants front of stage – as well as offering a view of the Rhine.

During construction there was very little space for storage; all deliveries of materials had to be timed precisely, staff could only reach the site by lift and a crane stood regularly in the middle of the pedestrian zone.

Project: Between Mainz Cathedral, the River Rhine and the Sky
Landscape architect:
Dieter Dirlenbach, dirlenbach – garten mit stil, Geisenheim
Photos: Andreas Gregory
Location: Mainz
www.garten-mit-stil.de

Vienna's inner city is its first municipal district and at the same time the historic heart of Austria's capital, in which 1,714,000 inhabitants live.
Population density:
5,599 inhabitants/km²

48° 12' N | 16° 22' E
Situated on the edge of the Vienna Woods, the climate transitions here from continental to oceanic. For Austria it is a relatively mild climate.
Height above sea level: 188 metres

The roof garden in the centre of Vienna was established for two neighbours who had befriended each other. The design was developed to suit both the clients and the genius loci.

In addition, there were two further determining factors: limits to what could be done in terms of construction as well as special legal conditions. The limited load-bearing capacity of the roof had to be taken into account just as much as the tenancy agreement that allows each tenant a terrace of only 25 m² and that nothing – whether plants, building or garden components – could be higher than 130 cm.
These limiting terms of reference were seen as a challenge and what was built was an especially spacious landscape using white quartz slabs, interspersed with intensively planted stainless steel troughs.

VIENNA
Inner City

The seating area is accessed by two separate wooden footbridges that are elevated up to 40 cm above the quartz landscape and watercourses.

A feeling of spaciousness is achieved through the planting. The planting concept is based around long strips that run the entire length of the terrace. Grasses are at the centre of the plantings. Ornamental onions *(Allium sphaerocephalon)* and perennials, such as geranium, continue the black-and-white theme.

Vienna's landmark, the Stephansdom, lies in direct view of the terrace. One of the essential tasks for the landscaper was to emphasise the cathedral, whilst at the same time creatively hinting at other areas that lay beyond what could be seen from the small terrace.

On the larger of the two terraces a watercourse rouses the visitor's curiosity, whilst at the same time bringing movement and freshness amongst the stone and wood.

Project: Riverscape
Landscape architect:
Clemens Lutz, Stalzer Lutz Gärten
Photos: Clemens Lutz
Location: Vienna, inner city
www.stalzerlutz.at

VIENNA
Mariahilf

Mariahilf is Vienna's sixth municipal district and, with an area of only 1.48 km², it is its second smallest.
Population density:
20,016 inhabitants/km²

48° 12' N | 16° 21' E
Located on the edge of the Vienna Woods, this area has a relatively mild but windy climate for Austria; within the district of Mariahilf there is a 30 m difference in height, making it Vienna's steepest district.
Height above sea level: 188 metres

The roof garden on top of a prestigious office expansion of a building from the late 19th century was designed using polygonal shapes. A multi-functional landscape that offered interesting views over the neighbouring museums and historical surroundings was created.
Local ash wood was used for the floor, seating, cladding and the formal divides in the planting beds. A wood of birch sticks *(Betula utilis)* created a screen for privacy, whilst at the same time creating a wind chime effect.
Unusual plant varieties with their unique shapes and colours break up the more formal geometric shapes. To give depth to the foliage the paperbark maple *(Acer griseum)*, green Japanese maple *(Acer palmatum 'Osakazuki')*, lemon-lime stag's horn sumac *(Rhus typhina 'Tiger Eyes')* and Bhutan pine *(Pinus wallichiana)* were all used. The ground planting used perennials such as Star of Persia *(Allium christophii)*, iris *(Iris barbata 'Night Owl')* and Mexican feather grass *(Stipa tenuissima)*.

Project: Mariahilferstrasse
Landscape architect:
Bernd Hochwartner, Walter Sulser – Weidlfein Gartenkunst
Photos:
Bernd Hochwartner, Walter Sulser
Location: Vienna-Mariahilf
www.weidlfein.com

ASIA

Project: Macao Arts Garden
Landscape architects:
Francisco Manuel Caldeira Cabral,
Elsa Maria Matos Severino,
Gabinete de Arquitectura Paisajista
Photos:
Francisco Manuel Caldeira Cabral

MACAU
Arts Garden

Macau, situated close to Hong Kong, is a former Portuguese colony with approximately 573,000 inhabitants. In 1999 it was incorporated into the People's Republic of China as a Special Administrative Region. Macau is connected to the mainland by a man-made causeway.
Population density:
20,319 inhabitants/km²

22° 12' N | 113° 33' E
Located at the mouth of the Pearl River Delta; sub-tropical climate, humid for 10 months of the year with up to 97 percent humidity. Monsoons are common from April to September. Constantly at threat from typhoons and tsunamis.
Height above sea level: 0–89 metres

An attractive park was to be created along the main street in the centre of Macau. Part of this commission was to complete a re-design of the

Macau Arts Garden on the 14,500 m² roof of the garage complex.

Amongst the casinos and heavy traffic of the city, a green oasis was to be created for the locals that invited them to enjoy a stroll or just quietly linger for a moment. The garden's concept was to create a fusion of Chinese and Western Portuguese cultures.

One of the main attractions of the roof garden are the trick fountains. They can perform a variety of different effects and interactive games. The burbling sounds of the fountains play a large part in the relaxing effect of the garden and, in addition, help to absorb some of the traffic noise.

Such roof gardens help to stem air pollution and make a significant contribution to increasing quality of life.

The active night life and the hot and humid climate make the roof garden especially attractive after dark. Its appearance at night with its illuminated fountains attracts a lot of attention. LED fittings ensure energy-saving lighting and a constantly changing play of colours through red, green and blue. The large areas of water and the cybernetic fountains with programmable jet nozzles combined with the light effects guarantee a spectacular water show.

All of these attractions are surrounded by thick vegetation that gives you the feeling of being in a much larger green space.

The garden itself encourages people to enjoy their night life outside. The strong presence of nature reinforced by intensive plantings of trees and shrubs has attracted many birds and insects so that a self-sustaining ecosystem has been created in the middle of the city.

Project: Macao Arts Garden
Landscape architects:
Francisco Manuel Caldeira Cabral,
Elsa Maria Matos Severino,
Gabinete de Arquitectura Paisajista
Photos:
Francisco Manuel Caldeira Cabral
Location: Macau
www.franciscocaldeiracabral.com

OSAKA
Namba Parks

Osaka has 2,670,730 inhabitants and is the third largest city and the traditional commercial centre of Japan. Population density: 12,024 inhabitants/km²

34° 39' 41'' N | 135° 30' 06'' E
Located on the western side of the main island of Honshu in the Bay of Osaka: warm temperate to sub-tropical climate. Typhoon season from September to October.
Height above sea level: 12 metres

The Namba Park, one of the largest roof gardens in Japan, was built over a 30-storey office tower and a 46-storey apartment building.

Here, the landscape architects Jerde saw nature as a form of urban intervention and have conceived this project as nature enriching the city to release it from its boundaries.

Namba Park, built as if on a hillside, can be seen from a long way away. It is a green oasis in a city in which any form of nature is rare.
Away from the hectic city life the park transports people into another world — a world with shadowy groves of trees, peaceful green spaces, relaxing waterfalls and fountains and terraces from which you can enjoy a view over the wide-ranging site and the city either alone or in company.

The challenge of this project was to create a living, green environment for a wide variety of uses – and yet always maintain a seamless connection with the main traffic hubs. The densely built-up area and the surrounding buildings precluded every form of natural landscaping or surroundings. This led to the idea of creating a terrain that resembled a canyon that ran over several storeys and through the entire building complex of Namba Park.

The path leads the visitor though a multitude of small valleys, over hills, into small coves or into secret places. On every level in selected places there is access to open-air terraces. Glass bridges connect both sides of the canyon and these are lit up at night using light arcs.

One of the main tasks of the project was to reduce the inner-city 'heat oasis' effect. Whilst in summer asphalt heats up to 51°C and concrete to 45°C, the temperature in Namba Park's roof gardens reaches a pleasant 34°C. The canyon-like construction contributes greatly to regulating the micro-climate that exists within Namba Park. In summer the canyon also provides natural ventilation and shade and acts as a heat shield.

In winter the loss of heat from the building is reduced thanks to the green roof areas. In addition, the noise reduction properties of the gardens also heighten the inhabitants' and visitors' wellbeing.

Namba Park's design incorporates ponds, fountains, trees, shrubs and flower beds.

70,000 plants and trees were necessary to cover the roof garden's area of 1.15 hectares in total. There are more than 300 different types of plants ranging from trees to herbs and spices, including climbing roses (Rosa sp.), glossy abelia (Abelia grandiflora), bonsai tree of a thousand stars (Serissa foetida), buddleia (Buddleja davidii), lavender (Lavandula angustifolia), oakleaf hydrangea (Hydrangea quercifolia), Persian silk tree (Albizia julibrissin), lamb's ears (Stachys byzantina), Japanese pepper bush (Clethra barbinervis), lobelia (different varieties of Lobelia), white butterfly ginger (Hedychium coronarium), silver thorn (Elaeagnus pungens) and rosemary (Rosmarius officinalis).

All of the green areas are irrigated using water recycled from the restaurants in the office complex.

Project: Namba Parks
Architecture, Design, Landscaping concept: The Jerde Partnership
Photos: Hiroyuki Kawano
Location: Osaka, Japan
www.jerde.com

The suburb of Ramat Aviv is in the north-west part of Tel Aviv's first district.
Population density:
5,576 inhabitants/km²

32° 06' 27'' N | 34° 47' 45'' E
Located on the Mediterranean: subtropical climate; in winter the temperature falls to about 12°C.
Height above sea level: 17 metres

Here, an old olive tree was accorded special honours. It was imported from Galilee and lifted up by crane to the roof terrace on the tenth storey. There, it was put in its own bed constructed from old bricks and provided with its own irrigation system. All of the other design features were built up around the olive tree which took centre stage. The Southern European character of the garden can also be seen in the furniture chosen. The roof garden runs around the entire apartment and the residents have a direct view out into the flourishing surroundings from each of the large windows. Like pictures on the wall, the garden is ever present in the apartment.

Project: Sade
Landscape architect: Gabi Garbi,
Yarok Landscape Culture
Photos: Gabi Garbi
Location: Ramat Aviv, Tel Aviv, Israel
www.yarok.com

TEL AVIV
Sade

TEL AVIV
Top of the World

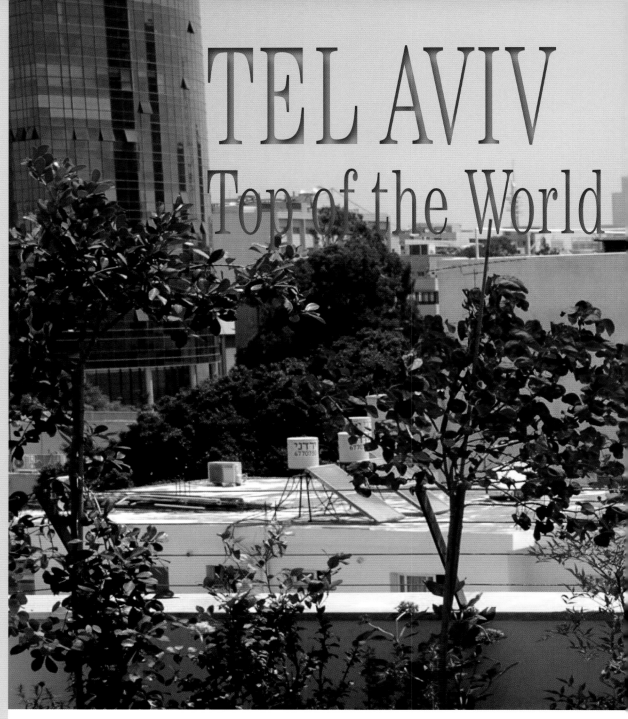

Tel Aviv-Jaffa, with 391,000 inhabitants, is Israel's second largest city.
Population density:
5,576 inhabitants/km²

32° 03' N | 34° 45' E
Situated on the Mediterranean: sub-tropical climate.
Height above sea level: 17 metres

The concept was to create a Mediterranean garden utilising material from the region as well as plants that were resistant to salt, wind and heat, such as lemon *(Citrus x limon)*, mandarin *(Citrus reticulata)*, olive *(Olea europaea)* and grapefruit *(Punica granatum)*. Fast-growing plants take over the function of screening for privacy with low rock garden plants and shrubs framing the view to the sea. All plants are irrigated by an automatic watering system.
25 tonnes of material were lifted up onto the roof garden by crane – soil, large stones, trees, building materials for the floors and ground surfaces. The terrace decks were elevated to create space for the soil needed to plant the olive trees.

Project: Top of The World in Tel-Aviv
Landscape architects:
Nili & Andy Darby Garden Design
Photos: Nili Lowicz-Darby
Location: Tel Aviv, Israel
www.darbydesigns.co.uk

SENTOSA
Sky Garden

Sentosa is a 5 km² island that is connected by a bridge to Singapore. Population density:
7,126 inhabitants/km²

1° 14' 51'' N | 103° 49' 49'' E
In the Straits of Singapore: tropical-humid climate, monsoons from October to February.
Height above sea level: 0–60 metres

Singapore, independent since 1965, is made up of 60 densely populated islands. The building plots on the island of Sentosa are not terribly large and neighbouring properties are all very close to one another.

The client wanted a modern, multistorey house with the living areas' privacy protected on the sides from people being able to see in.

The front and back of the four-storey house was terraced to allow for each level having some interaction with its own garden area. Thus, everyone living in the property, regardless of which storey they are in, will feel as if they are at ground level, surrounded by a flourishing garden with generous lawned spaces.

And Singapore helps with exactly the right climate for tropical greenery, colourful seas of flowers and lush 'English' lawn.

The consistent, tropical climate guarantees an average temperature of 27°C, with humidity on a dry day reaching at least 65 percent and brief but heavy showers looking after year-round natural irrigation.

Thanks to its weeping stems, which look as if it is raining flowers, orange flowering tropical ornamental bushes, fire-cracker ferns (Russelia equiseti-formis) positioned on the edges of the terraces create a soft yet striking transition to the living areas underneath as well as the surroundings.

Impressive palms, richly blooming rhododendron, single and shaped trees attract the attention on all levels of the garden. The green roof of the 'Sky garden' house ensures a pleasantly cool temperature in the house's living areas.

This project shows that you can have all of the advantages of a roof garden as part of a luxurious family home without having to be on the top of a skyscraper.

Project: Sky Garden House
Architect:
Guz Wilkinson – Guz Architects
Photos: Patrick Bingham Hall
Location:
Island of Sentosa, Singapore
www.guzarchitects.com

Shanghai, with around 23 million inhabitants, is the most significant industrial city of the People's Republic of China.
Population density:
3,630 inhabitants/km²

31° 14' N | 121° 28' E
Located at the mouth of the Yangtze River on the East China Sea: subtropical maritime climate with four clearly defined seasons.
Height above sea level: 4 metres

A large roof together with two huge load-bearing cylinders forms the structure of the building. Two cylinders in the inside of the pavilion and the view of the roof from below comprise the urban space.

Complemented by the flow of visitors through the exhibition area in the cylinder and on several ramps at different levels, as well as the multifunctional stage and the restaurant, this urban space is both physically and acoustically condensed. With its hard, angular surface areas and its distinguishing characteristics – loud, shadowy and active – it stirs the Yin.

Counter and complementary to the urban space, the green cylinder and the roof create a calm, open and light landscape that stands for the Yang. The element that links the two spaces is the cable car. It takes the visitors out of the 'city' and into 'nature' and then back again.

The outside space is a collage of fragments of what would make up a typical Swiss landscape. It starts when the cable car begins to climb up through a canyon lined with dense and lush ferns and grasses. The dripping water collects in large water basins that take up the entire floor of the cylinder. As you rise up out of the cylinder it gets lighter and quieter with wide-ranging views into the distance. The visitor is now carried over hilly 'mountain pastures' and fields before it descends once more into a canyon.

The Swiss pavilion's architecture embodies a symbiosis of city and countryside. It presents itself as a hybrid of technology and nature uniting a rural and urban existence whilst maintaining a balance.

Project: Urban and Rural Interaction, Swiss Pavilion at EXPO 2010
Architect: Buchner Bründler Architects, Basel, www.bbarc.ch
Landscape architecture: Fontana Landscape architecture, Basel, www.fontana-la.ch
Photos: Raphael Suter, Basel; Markus Koepfli; Arnd Dewald; Iwan Baan, Amsterdam

SINGAPORE
Cluny House

Singapore, with around 5,076,700 inhabitants, is in terms of area the smallest country in South-East Asia. Population density: 7,126 inhabitants/km²

1° 17' N | 103° 50' E
Located on the main island between Malaysia and Indonesia: tropical-humid climate; the temperature is more than 28°C for almost the entire year.

This environmentally friendly house was constructed around a large area of water which forms the centre of the property.

Lushly planted roof gardens surround the inner courtyard and give the residents the feeling that nature is present everywhere in the house.

It might not be obvious, but Cluny House is a modern high-tech building.
A photovoltaic plant is used to passively cool the house down in an energy-saving way. Solar panels heat the water. Rainwater is collected in tanks on the roof and then sterilised and reused.

Environmentally friendly materials such as recycled teak and artificial wood create a comfortable surrounding without endangering the limited local resources.

The planting reflects the diversity of the tropical plant world. Tree ferns *(Cyatheales)*, bamboo *(Bambusa)*, russelia *(Russelia)*, frangipani *(Plumeria)* and palms can be found here as well as bougainvillea *(Bougainvillia)* and other fast-growing climbing plants.

This project brings technology, function and design in close communion with nature – creating a comfortable, luxurious and enduring family home.

Project: Cluny House
Landscape architect:
Guz Wilkinson, Guz Architects
Photos: Patrick Bingham Hall
Location: Singapore
www.guzarchitects.com

AUSTRALIA

Project: Freshwater Place
Landscape architect:
Lawrence Blyton
Photos: Stuart Tyler

Melbourne is the second largest city in Australia after Sydney, with approximately 3.4 million inhabitants. According to surveys conducted by *The Economist* over successive years, it has been considered to be the most liveable city in the world.
Population density:
1,978 inhabitants/km²

37° 48' S | 144° 57' E
Located on the Yarra River: temperate climate.
Height above sea level: 14 metres

Freshwater is a luxurious housing complex built on the banks of the Yarra River in the centre of Melbourne. The roof garden on the tenth floor provides the residents with an oasis in the centre of the city with places for rest and relaxation, as well as providing somewhere from which to enjoy the unique view over Melbourne. The garden is an especially popular location for seeing in the New Year. The aim of the design was to create an aesthetically pleasing space for the residents to enjoy.

Melbourne's climate can be very changeable – its inhabitants, called Melbournians, often talk about there being 'four seasons in one day'. The often extreme climatic conditions that Melbourne experiences can pose a great challenge for roof gardens.

Plants typically used on Australian lawns, such as Kikuyu grass *(Pennisetum clandestinum)*, had to be planted out on a special growing medium with a soil depth of 25–35 cm to survive the high summer temperatures, dry conditions and storms. For trees such as the Manchurian pear *(Pyrus ussuriensis)*, the depth was increased to 75 cm. The substrata mix consisted of sand, water-absorbent flakes and bark mulch.

The annual growth rate of the plants is monitored regularly and the fertiliser dosage rates are then adjusted accordingly.

Project: Freshwater Place
Greening technology:
Fytogreen Australia Pty Ltd
Landscape architect:
Lawrence Blyton
Photos: Stuart Tyler
Location: Melbourne
www.fytogreen.com.au

MELBOURNE
Freshwater Place

SYDNEY
Office

Sydney is the capital of the Australian state of New South Wales. With around 4 million inhabitants, it is the largest city on the Australian continent.
Population density:
2,188 inhabitants/km²

33° 52' S | 151° 12' E
Subtropical climate moderated by its proximity to the coast; the lowest temperature ever measured is 2.1°C.
Height above sea level: 17 metres

This roof garden belongs to the head office of a well-known company. They were seeking an open-air space that was suitable for both large and small corporate events.

The design transformed the generously sized terrace into a comfortable and versatile space that offered areas for more intimate gatherings as well as room for larger social events. In the evening, the lighting system that is installed gives the garden a calm and relaxed atmosphere.
The challenge of this garden came from having to transport all of the building materials by crane up to its almost inaccessible location. To do this, they had to temporarily shut a busy street.

Before construction started, the entire area was covered with water-impermeable sheeting.

When choosing the plants and materials for the garden, the extreme climatic conditions had to be considered.

The plantings of strelitzia *(Strelitzia reginae)*, rubber plant *(Ficus elastica)*, hardy common box *(Buxus sempervirens)* and other topiary species require limited maintenance.

Project:
Corporate Office – Roof Garden
Landscape architect:
William Dangar, Dangar Group
Photos: Chris Warnes
Location: Martin Place, Sydney
www.dangargroup.com

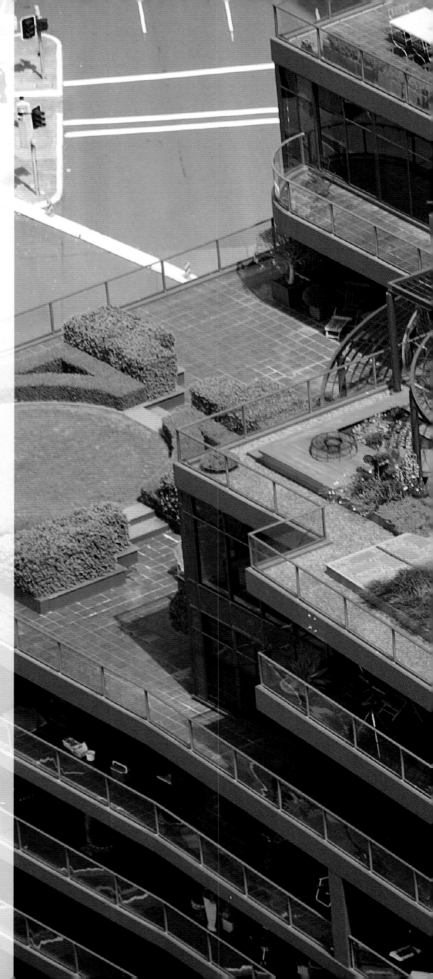

SYDNEY
Penthouse

The Sydney suburb located at the foot of the Sydney Harbour Bridge and known as The Rocks is where the city was founded and thus is one of the oldest parts of the city. It is also one of the most visited parts of Sydney. Population density: 2,188 inhabitants/km²

33° 51' S | 151° 12' E
Located on the east coast of Australia on the Pacific Ocean: subtropical climate.
Height above sea level: 3 metres

From this penthouse located 27 floors above the city you can enjoy a breath-taking view over Sydney.

The client that commissioned this roof garden over two levels is a businessman who frequently travels away from home on business but has his office at home.
He wanted an attractive garden that was suitable for business receptions as well as providing him with a quiet open-air space in which to work or relax.

Before work started, the terraces were unattractive and largely unused. The second level could only be reached via an emergency fire escape ladder.

Due to the strict building regulations, the architect had to work closely with the building's management in order that the design and construction could be carried out as required. Special care also had to be taken since all of the building materials had to be lifted up onto the terrace and constructed in situ.

The result for the client was a quiet garden featuring ponds and fish. The open spaces can be reached from the bedroom as well as the other living spaces.

Much attention was paid to the quality of the workmanship of the individual elements. Wooden bridges connect all of the seating areas, whilst at the same time inviting the user to discover and enjoy the surrounding living space. When choosing the plants for the garden particular emphasis was placed on cloud-like, soft structures and rounded form. Planting containers surround the ponds and cover the majority of the lower level.

The plant beds are less than 30 cm deep and they are prevented from becoming waterlogged by the use of drainage cells that the water can run off into. A spiral staircase connects the two levels.

The upper level is designed for entertaining, with lounge areas, shady places, a spa pool and sun loungers. Wood dominates here as the main design element. Robust and heat-tolerant plants are used in isolation to effect and are also used to form dense cloud-shaped carpets.
In the evening a well-thought-out lighting system bestows the roof terrace with a special ambience.

The entire construction has been built as a modular system with each element measuring 2 x 2 metres. None of the parts was allowed to be permanently fixed to the building's structure. This fact means that the entire garden could, if necessary, be moved to a different location. During construction special care had to be taken – any component falling from the twenty-seventh floor could have had fatal consequences.

What is so special about this roof garden is that whilst, on the one hand, it is built for relaxing, at the same time it offers the perfect setting for parties – moreover, against a stunning backdrop.

Project: Sydney Penthouse
Landscape Designer: Matthew
Cantwell, Secret Gardens of Sydney

Photos: Peter Brennan
Location: Sydney
www.secretgardens.com.au

Sydney is the capital of the Australian state of New South Wales. With its 4 million inhabitants, it is not only the largest city on the Australian continent but also the trade and financial centre of the country.
Population density:
2,188 inhabitants/km²

33° 51' S | 151° 12' E
Located on Australia's east coast on the Pacific Ocean.
Height above sea level: 3 metres

This ultimate in secret gardens lies hidden on the twenty-fifth floor of an apartment building in Sydney. The client wanted a garden that was traditionally planted and yet was designed to suit the available space and the building itself.

In this way the architecture could be highlighted and complemented and not hidden. The terraced areas were meant to facilitate relaxing outdoors as well as providing the perfect location for larger parties.

The green sculptured garden is surrounded by several skyscrapers. The original planting, which was comprised of hedges that blocked the view from both inside and out, was replaced with new, lower borders. These allowed the owners to enjoy fantastic views over the city.

Box cut into cone shapes and hedges created the formal and linear elements of the garden, whilst free-growing iris and lavender broke up the severity. Wooden seating around the edges of the garden frame it and offer places to sit and relax.

The strict conditions surrounding the building of this garden meant that little consideration could be given to using real grass. The central circle of artificial grass gives the feeling of real grass but without the associated need for maintenance and watering.

Once again, a modular system was used during construction. None of the parts could be attached to the building itself. All of the building materials were transported onto the roof using the lift and then put together on the roof terrace.

'The focus of this rooftop garden is' on the creation of 'a formal, whimsical outdoor entertaining area.'

Project: Sydney – Secret Garden
Landscape Designer: Matthew Cantwell, Secret Gardens of Sydney

AMERICA

Project: Roof Garden on the Atlantic
Landscape architects:
Francisco Manuel Caldeira Cabral,
Elsa Maria Matos Severino –
Gabinete de Arquitecture Paisagista
Architect: Sylvia Almeida Braga
Photos:
Francisco Manuel Caldeira Cabral

ANGRA dos REIS
Atlantic Garden

Angra dos Reis is a Brazilian city with 170,000 inhabitants located on the coast at the southern end of the state of Rio de Janeiro.
Population density:
180 inhabitants/km²

23° 1' S | 44° 19' W
Located on the Atlantic coast: tropical climate with a constant trade wind.
Height above sea level: 6 metres

This private estate lies on a small hill in Angra dos Reis between the Atlantic rainforest (Mata Atlantica) and the ocean in one of the most beautiful and scenic parts of Brazil. In designing the buildings for this

location, the architect, Sylvia Almeida Braga, hid the majority of the structures in order to show respect for the genius loci, the local spirit of the area. The unusual concept not only shows great respect for the natural setting but also inspired the landscape architects.

When you step onto the property you do not see the buildings at all. It is possible to identify the shape and detail of the landscape as well as several works of art. The entrance too is sunken, as if it were a jungle grotto, reached over a suspended wooden bridge. The challenge for the landscape architect was to reconstruct the landscape and incorporate

an art collection whilst coping with the sloping nature of the site.

The entire garden covered an area of 4,500 m², of which 750 m² covered the majority of the main building's roof as well as the entire roof of the guest house.

On the main building there are two formal seating areas positioned in strategic locations that are reached over a meandering path made from slabs of black slate set into a bed of white gravel.

Planting the dunes with white striped bamboo (*Pleioblastus variegatus* 'Fortunei'), feathertop and fountain grass (*Pennisetum villosum, P. setaceum*) and Chinese silver

grass (*Miscanthus sinensis* 'Zebrinus') brings natural accents and movement into the new landscape. Scented plants such as frangipani (*Plumeria rubra, P. rubra fo. acutifolia*) and night-blooming jasmine (*Cestrum nocturnum*) also play important roles.

Smaller flowering shrubs and trees such as crepe myrtle (*Lagerstroemia*), glory bush (*Tibouchina*) and the coral tree (*Erythrina*) defy the strong sea winds. They blend in with high surrounding trees such as African tulip trees (*Spathodea*), tabebuia or trumpet trees (*Tabebuia*), orchid trees (*Bauhinia*) and other rainforest trees. Shrubs were planted around the feet of the palm trees that are

so typical of this tropical region, which ensured that they were integrated into the garden's ecosystem. Bismarck palms (*Bismarckia nobilis*) impress with their gigantic, grey-green leaves, as do the red sealing wax palms (*Cyrtostachys renda*) with their shiny red stalks.

Project: Roof Garden on the Atlantic
Landscape architects:
Francisco Manuel Caldeira Cabral,
Elsa Maria Matos Severino –
Gabinete de Arquitecture Paisagista
Architect: Sylvia Almeida Braga
Photos:
Francisco Manuel Caldeira Cabral
Location: Angra dos Reis, Brazil
www.franciscocaldeiracabral.com

CHICAGO
Youth Center

With a population of approximately 2,700,000, Chicago in the state of Illinois is the third largest city in the USA.
Population density:
4,582 inhabitants/km²

41° 45' 49'' N | 87° 36' 08'' W
Located on the south west bank of Lake Michigan: continental climate with hot summers and cold winters.
Height above sea level: 182 metres

The roof garden of the Gary Comer Youth Center was established to provide afternoon care for the children and young people of the surrounding neighbourhoods who had no access at home to gardens or nature. Over 500 kg of organic fruit and vegetables are harvested every year.

After harvest the produce is used by the school pupils in local restaurants or in the school's own cafeteria.

The 760 m² roof garden is an example of how an otherwise little utilised space can be put to sensible use for both urban cultivation and education and in attractively designed surroundings.

An important concern was the safety of pupils in both the garden area and surrounding building. The architectural concept created an enclosed green space in which the young people could plan and enjoy their time outside.

In order to be able to actively grow vegetables on this area a soil depth of 40–60 cm was required. This ensures that there is no damage done to the superstructure underneath.

A permanent gardener is employed who is also responsible for the creative education programme as well as the ongoing care and maintenance of the garden.

The roof garden is located above the second storey of the school and is surrounded by corridors and classrooms on the third floor.

Its sheltered location creates a mild micro-climate so that even in winter the garden can continue to be cultivated and crops can be harvested from it. The roof garden represents the practical implementation of a policy of protecting both the environment and the climate as it helps to save energy by limiting the amount of heat that the building loses.

For the pupils it offers a welcome break from the usual routine of lessons by providing them with an open-air classroom and direct access to nature.

Project:
Gary Comer Youth Center –
Green Roof
Landscape architect:
Hoerr Schaudt Landscape Architects
Photos: Scott Shigley
Location: Chicago, USA
www.hoerrschaudt.com

HOUSTON
Greenbriar

With approximately 2,100,000 inhabitants, Houston is the largest city in Texas and the third largest in the USA.
Population density:
1,399 inhabitants/km²

29° 42' 34'' N | 95° 23' 54'' W
Situated on the Gulf of Mexico; warm and humid climate with hot summers and cool winters.
Height above sea level: 12 metres

The Greenbriar Rooftop Garden project was built on the virtually unused roof of the Houston Medical Center's car park.

The roof garden is 550 m² in size and offers a variety of open spaces which, due to the diverse structure, textures and planting used, can all be put to separate use. Sun sails mark the places where people can gather and sit together, whilst loungers located in a Zen-like pebble garden invite you to relax. A circular copse of bamboo *(Bambus multiplex 'Alphonse Karr')* surrounds a mirror-smooth circular pool – this place is ideal for spending time in meditation and contemplation.

Every morning yoga classes are held in one area planted out with drought-resistant Bermuda or dog's tooth grass *(Cynodon dactylon)*. During the day, many patients enjoy walking here barefoot.

The design takes into account that in this location, only drought-tolerant plants will really ever flourish. Yellow peacock flowers *(Dietes bicolor)*, red fountain grass *(Pennisetum setaceum* 'Rubrum') and common horsetail *(Equisetum arvense)* are all grown in the one-metre-high planters.

Perforated metal panels are covered with fibreglass. At night when these are lit from the inside they look like Japanese lanterns. The roof garden was created for the Houston Medical Center's patients and their families. Ramps ensure that every part of the garden can be reached without any problems. Everyone can find a quiet place in this garden without having to leave the city.

Like others, this roof garden also benefits the environment. It stores rainwater and reduces the 'heat oasis' effect; and its plants help to clean the air and offer a natural refuge for birds as they migrate across Texas.

Project: Greenbriar Rooftop Garden
Landscape architects: Rame &
Russell Hruska – Intexure Architects
Photos: Intexure Architects
Location: Houston, Texas
www.intexure.com

NEW YORK
Rockefeller

Around 1.7 million inhabitants live in the New York borough of Manhattan. Population density: 27,476 inhabitants/km²

40° 45' 31" N | 73° 58' 45" W
Manhattan is an island at the mouth of the Hudson River: mild climate. Height above sea level: 0–80 metres

The Rockefeller Center in the New York borough of Manhattan comprises a group of 21 high-rise buildings.
The roof gardens were completed in 1936 after three years construction. John R. Todd and the architect, Raymond Hood, were the leading visionaries behind this roof garden project. The Rockefeller Center was thus the first private building with extensive gardens created on both street and roof level.

The two planners, Todd and Hood, believed that architectural design should offer something to both the tenants and the passers-by and so installed 'hanging gardens' as a treat for the eyes of the thousands of people working in the Rockefeller Center. Four roof gardens were created along Fifth Avenue, each with a theme that fitted the building on which it was located; the garden on the Palazza d'Italia is surrounded by paving stones that came from Italy, including two flagstones that came from the Roman Forum; the tables on the British Empire Building are covered with sun umbrellas and the residents can enjoy their five o'clock tea hidden away behind hedges.

One of the roof gardens – 620 Loft & Garden – can be hired for events. Surrounded by a classically formal garden it enjoys an unforgettable view over the neo-gothic Saint Patrick's Cathedral.

Project:
Rockefeller Center Rooftop Gardens
Architects:
John R. Todd and Raymond Hood
Photo: Michelle Rago design
Location: Manhattan, New York City
www.rockefellercenter.com

NEW YORK

High Line

With more than 8,175,000 inhabitants, New York City has the highest density of population of any of the cities in the USA.
Population density:
10,356 inhabitants/km²

40° 44' 46" N | 74° 0' 22" W
Located on the east coast of America in the New York Bay, its weather is influenced by the continental landmass to the west: moderate climate with tropically warm summers and cold winters.
Height above sea level: 10 metres

The New Yorker High Line was built in 1930.

The elevated railway line was built to run between apartment blocks on stilts of between five and nine metres in height and with a width of 9 to 18 metres. Freight trains ran along the 2.33-km-long stretch of track for 50 years before the line was decommissioned and forgotten.

In December 2002 the then mayor, Michael Bloomberg, declared it to be a site of historical importance and a preservation order was placed on it. Architects and landscape gardeners competed to win the contract for the 'floating gardens'.

The planners wanted to maintain the site's 'wilderness'-like character

as well as its natural flora that had flourished over the 20 years of neglect. The tracks themselves were to remain visible to preserve and remind people of its historic origins.

Field Operations developed a planking system for the pathways, consisting of smooth tapered concrete planks with edges that come to a point on the side so that after planting the edges between the hard concrete and the soft plantings started to blur.

The design of the park provided for a wide variety of plantings, ranging from very damp, moor-like areas through to parts containing arid steppe grasses. ZinCo Floradrain components were installed for the drainage system on what is probably the longest roof garden in the world.

The profiled drainage components have troughs on the top which catch rainwater. Any excess water is carried off along the channels than run underneath the drainage system.

Where freight trains once ran it isn't now just the New Yorkers who walk, sit in the sun and enjoy the view of the Empire State Building, Hudson River and Statue of Liberty. For visitors from all over the world the High Line has become a 'must see' attraction from both a town planning and garden landscaping point of view.

The organisation 'Friends of the High Line' now controls about 90 percent of the finances for the High Line project and is responsible for the management and maintenance of the park.

The 'green' concept that lies behind the High Line park is inspiring similar projects around the world.

Town planners from Rotterdam, Hong Kong, Singapore and Jerusalem have already visited the tracks.

In Chicago a disused railway line is to be turned into a green space. There are ongoing discussions in Philadelphia about transforming an 18-metre-high viaduct, and in Atlanta they are to build a green belt on a railway that runs for 35 km around the inner city.

Project: High Line
Planting technology: ZinCo GmbH
Landscape architects: James Corner, Field Operations and Piet Oudolf
Photos: ZinCo, Kathrin Huemer
Location: New York City
www.zinco-greenroof.com

SAN FRANCISCO
City Roof Garden

With 805,235 inhabitants, San Francisco is the fourth largest city in the USA.
Population density:
6,654 inhabitants/km²

37° 47' N | 122° 25' W
Situated on the Pacific with a Mediterranean climate; in summer there is virtually no rain and in winter it is mild with plenty of rain.
Height above sea level: 16 metres

Here, the client wanted to add a bright and colourful green space to his urban loft. Since there was no other available space a section of the roof of a multi-storey car park was transformed into a roof garden. Areas that could later be extended were laid down for vegetables. The comfortable seating area is hidden away behind colourfully planted containers that also form a much-needed windbreak.

The permitted roof load demanded a rethink of the choice of planting medium to be used, so instead of soil a light perlite mix was used.

The plants that were chosen for the garden had to be salt- and drought-tolerant and be able to stand up to wind. Bamboo, Chinese silver grass *(Miscanthus sinensis)* and perennials such as kangaroo paw *(Anigozanthos)* and several shrubs form the permanent planting.

Annuals can be swapped at any time to match a new colour scheme. A large sun umbrella is indispensable in the summer months.

Project: City Roof Garden
Landscape architects:
Jude Hellewell & Laura White –
Outer Space Landscape Architecture
Photos: Jude Hellewell
Location: San Francisco
www.outerspacela.com

TORONTO
Carport

With 2.5 million inhabitants, Toronto is the largest Canadian city.
Population density:
4,207 inhabitants/km²

43° 40' 37'' N | 79° 23' 49'' W
Located in the far south of the country on the north west shore of Lake Ontario: in comparison with the rest of Canada a very mild climate with short, cold winters.
Height above sea level:
76–120 metres

These clients wanted not only to talk about 'greening' up our environment but wanted to turn their green thoughts into reality in the urban centre of Toronto. Thus, they resolved to create a roof garden on top of a carport behind their house.

In addition, the walnut tree *(Juglans regia)* that already stood in the backyard was to be given a new role and shelter the family's 'ultimate' tree house with its dense crown of foliage.

The planning authorities did not grant permission for a spiral staircase that was part of the original design, so instead of this a ladder now provides the access to the roof garden.
The innovation of this project lies in the way that a carport could be newly defined as the basis for a roof garden. Unused areas were transformed into a multi-functional space without requiring an extension. Using materials from around the region, an ecologically sound habitat was created for butterflies and other insects.

Steel, concrete and hardy lapacho wood *(Tabebuia ipe, Green Ironwood, Ipé)* were used to build the roof garden. As the name Ironwood suggests, this is an exceedingly heavy and du-

rable wood that is ideal for outside use.

A frame was incorporated into the back wall of the carport in which candles can be placed to create a welcoming and cosy atmosphere. The effect of the concrete and wood elements that might appear to be harsh are softened by the planting of fast-growing ornamental grasses, ivy, box hedges, Japanese ornamental maple and succulent flowering perennials *(Sedum)*. Limestone slabs in the roof garden connect it optically with the courtyard below.

At twilight and in the evening the lighting is an important aspect of the design as it contributes to the ambience.

Project: Carport & Green Roof
Designer: Cecconi Simone Inc.
Photos: Joy von Tiedemann
Location: Toronto, Ontario, Canada
www.cecconisimone.com

TORONTO
City Hall

With around 2.5 million inhabitants, Toronto is the largest city in Canada and the capital of the province of Ontario.
Population density:
4,207 inhabitants/km²

43° 39' 11'' N | 79° 23' 02'' W
Located in the far south of the country on the north west banks of Lake Ontario: in comparison with the rest of Canada, Toronto has a very mild climate with short, cold winters.
Height above sea level: 101 metres

The size of Toronto City Hall's Podium on Nathan Phillips Square, which was completed in 1965, is approximately 11,000 m².
Originally designed to be used for events and celebrations, the citizens of Toronto never really took to the expanse of concrete that formed the Podium and it was closed off to public access for more than ten years.

Today, following a model revitalisation, the Podium is Canada's largest publicly accessible roof garden and is viewed as the forerunner of all of the green roofs that are now following its example in Toronto.
The garden now fills the function for which the space was originally designed – it has become a popular location for weddings, events and large-scale mobile art installations, whilst at the same time being used as somewhere for people to enjoy a quiet moment by themselves.

Now on the roof garden and inspired by Paul Klee's Polyphony, there is a mosaic of 23 different varieties of sedum, mixed in with 42 different grasses as well as bulbs and tubers. The colours of the flowers change from bright yellow and orange in the southwest to red and purple in the northeast. The area that surrounds and frames the central council chamber is paved in black granite.

Just as in the case of most roof gardens, this one additionally helps the energy efficiency of the building. The roof membrane also helps to extend the life of the roof's construction and the plants act as air filters, reduce traffic noise and also offer a sustainable solution for the management of the building's storm-water.

This roof garden is a living space in the middle of a city dominated by concrete and buildings and helps to make the urban population more aware of environmental concerns.

Project: Toronto City Hall,
Podium Green Roof Garden
Landscape architects:
PLANT Architect Inc.
Photos: Steven Evans, Chris Pommer
Location: Nathan Phillips Square, Toronto
www.branchplant.com

NEW YORK

Trump Tower

Thanks

More than 700 people were contacted in the course of writing this book. Suggestions and tips that came from designers, architects and landscape designers – often despite language barriers – on four continents have been included in this book.

I would like to particularly thank those who provided editorial contributions, fascinating photos and detailed descriptions of the projects for the more than 40 inspiring roof gardens portrayed here. The result is an international overview of considerable breadth, showing how public and private green spaces can be designed and brought into being.

My thanks are also directed to those who showed understanding for the fact that their projects did not make the final cut and were not one of those chosen to feature here – although their work is worthy of being brought to the attention of a wider public.

Special thanks go to my teacher and supporter, Professor Franz Bódi, at the Higher Technical and Research Institute for Horticulture in Vienna-Schönbrunn.

I would like to thank my family for their moral support; Ulrich Hantsch for photo editing and my publisher for making my book a reality.